Treble viol

Tenor viola da gamba

Bass viola da gamba

Alto viol

—moveable frets

Viola d'amo

16th and 17th century Viol family instruments

Early harp

Psaltery

Lutes of the 17th century

lute back

10 string Guitar

Lutes and plucked string instruments

Zither

Early woodwind instruments

cap

Shawm, double-reed pipe

reeds — Crumhorn, double-reed pipe (cap removed)

Chalumeau, single-reed pipe

Transverse (side-held) flute

Recorder, pipe flute

Bass recorder

Brass instruments

Tambourine

17th century trumpets

Drums

Crook horn

Bells

Early trombones

Tabor, small drum

Early percussion instruments

An Introduction to Musical Instruments and the Symphony Orchestra

The Story of the

Incredible Orchestra

For my grammar school violin teacher.
—B.K.

The text of this book is set in 16-point Bembo.
The illustrations are ink and watercolor on paper.

Library of Congress Cataloging-in-Publication Data

Koscielniak, Bruce.
The story of the incredible orchestra / Bruce Koscielniak.
p.   cm.
Summary: Describes the orchestra, the families of instruments of which it is
made, and the individual instruments in each family.
ISBN 0-395-96052-5
1. Orchestra — Juvenile literature. 2. Musical instruments — Juvenile literature.
[1. Orchestra. 2. Musical instruments.]   I. Title.
ML 1200.K67   2000
784.2 — dc21   98-43933   CIP AC MN

Printed in Singapore
TWP 10 9 8 7 6 5 4 3 2 1

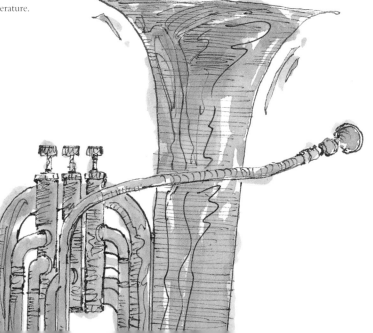

An Introduction to Musical Instruments and the Symphony Orchestra

The Story of the
Incredible Orchestra

by Bruce Koscielniak

Houghton Mifflin Company
Boston 2000

On   Volume
Off   Channel

W E'VE ALL SEEN AND HEARD ORCHESTRAS PERFORM, whether on television or in a live concert.

An orchestra, of course, is a big, often loud gathering of a great variety of musical instruments belonging to the string, woodwind, brass, and percussion families; it is led by a conductor who helps the musicians all play together.

But how did this wonderful gathering of sounds made by blowing air, bowing or plucking strings, and beating drums come about?

Tooters, Strings, and Beaters

No Orchestras Before 1600?

Before about 1600, instrumental musical groups were small ensembles of string, pipe, and beater instruments. Written music did not specify which instruments were to be used, and early instruments were not yet standard in shape, size, or in the way they were played.

Viols, lutes, harps, and zithers used gut strings, made of dried animal intestines, which produced a soft sound when played. This sound was perfect for indoor concerts but not very dynamic outdoors or in a large space such as a church.

Viol: An early string instrument

Recorder: A wooden pipe flute, similar in shape and size to the chalumeau but does not have a reed

Lute: A plucked instrument that has frets, a gourdlike sound box, and twelve or more strings

Guitar: A string instrument with frets (ridges set across the neck that serve to shorten the strings and change the notes), its six strings are plucked with the fingers or with a pick called a plectrum

Tambourine: A small drum with metal rattles in the frame

Early harps were small upright instruments that had thirty or more strings running from the neck to the soundboard that were played with the fingers.
Harp
Viola d'amore: A high-pitched viol
Chalumeau: Single-reed pipe
neck
sound box
PASTORAL
MUSICA
Zither
Zither: An instrument with a flat sound box and thirty to forty strings plucked with the fingers or a small pick made of wood or shell; some zithers also have frets to help create melody
Bass viol: An early string instrument with a range similar to the cello

The Orchestra Is Born!

In 1597, Giovanni Gabrieli (1557–1612), organist at St. Mark's Cathedral in Venice, Italy, wrote a piece of music called the *Sacrae Symphoniae* with separate parts for specific groups of instruments. Gabrieli was fond of combining such instruments as deep-toned trombones, brassy trumpets (which at this time had no valves), and strings to produce a powerful "chorus" of sound that would easily fill a soaring space. This assembly of instrument groups with different parts to play was the first orchestra!

Trombone

slide section

Early long trumpet

Trombone means "large trumpet" in Italian.

The Orchestra Arrives
With a Chorus of Sound

The trombone is a large trumpet-like instrument with a U-shaped slide added to lengthen the tubing and change the notes. In the Middle Ages the trombone was also called a sackbut.

Up to this point, trumpets had been used mainly for pageants and military music.

strings

Valveless trumpets

Slide trombones

The Baroque Period 1600-1750
Music with a Regular Pulse

In the Baroque period of music, orchestras typically remained small—suited to chamber playing as well as to larger outdoor performances.

Johann Sebastian Bach (1685–1750) wrote many instrumental works called concertos, suites, and sonatas for the Baroque orchestra. These musical pieces, each having several varied sections, usually feature a continuous bass part called *basso continuo* that is often played on bass string instruments. Harmonies above the bass line were written for harpsichord, recorder, strings, or any instruments the composer wanted to use and had available players for.

Baroque orchestras varied according to the instruments called for and the purpose of the music.

Oboes

Horn

Trumpets

Transverse (side-held) flutes

In early orchestras, one musician might act as music leader, helping to keep everyone playing together.

Concertos: Musical pieces that feature individual instruments playing with orchestral accompaniment

Suites: Compositions that consist of a series of instrumental dances

Sonatas: Musical works for one to four players

Violins

Recorders

Quill plectrum Harpsichord

Bach

When a harpsichord key is pressed, a wooden jack with a quill plectrum (the hard, hollow point of a feather shaft) is raised to pluck (pull and release) the string.

Viola da gamba: A bass viol

Violins in the Air

The Violin Family

Viol instruments, having six or more strings and frets, were often used in the Baroque period. However, by the early 1600s, violin makers were producing fine violins, violas, and cellos. These instruments all belong to the violin family and have four strings and no frets. In northern Italy, the Amati family and their famous apprentice Antonio Stradivari (1644–1737) crafted violin instruments that produced such pleasing tones that by 1750 they had replaced the somewhat nasal-sounding viols. Of the many fine violin makers of this period, Antonio Stradivari is considered to have brought violin making to its pinnacle with instruments that were and still are highly prized for beautiful workmanship, responsiveness to a skilled player, and superb tone.

The body of the instrument is called the sound box.

scroll

tuning pegs

neck and fingerboard

bridge

f-hole

Violin: Smallest, highest-pitched member of the violin family

V.Ki ♡

Viola: A little larger and deeper in tone than the violin

Frog: A small wooden handle on the grip of the bow that moves by means of the set screw to tighten and loosen the bowhairs

A violin bow is made of a slender, slightly curved stick strung with a thin ribbon of stretched horsehair.

bowhairs

A hard, yellow tree resin product called rosin is applied to the bowhairs to make them sticky enough to pull the strings when the bow is drawn over them.

ROSIN

The bow makes the strings vibrate to produce sound in the instrument. Sound comes out of the f-holes.

The bridge carries string vibration to the sound box.

Cello: Much larger than the viola, it produces a rich, mellow tone

Double bass: The largest member of the string family, this instrument has a very deep tone

Shawm: An early double-reed pipe that was a forerunner of the oboe

The Outstanding Oboes
A New Wind

reeds

Oboe double reed

silk thread

cork cover over metal tube fits into oboe

folded cane reed (folded end is trimmed off to produce two matching reeds)

reed

bent crook

English horn

Double-reed Woodwinds

Around 1650, a new instrument appeared on the music scene—the oboe. The name "oboe" comes from the French *hautbois,* which means "high wood." It is a double-reed instrument with a high mellow tone that made it an immediate favorite with audiences. Along with violins and flutes, most orchestras had to have at least a pair of these new oboes.

The deeper-toned English horn, also a double-reed instrument, has a pear-shaped bell at its end and is really a larger version of the oboe which requires the same fingering.

The oboe has three sections of wood tube.

Fluttering reeds cause the air in the instrument to vibrate to produce sound.

The flare end of a woodwind or brass instrument is called the bell.

The oboe was developed in France by the Hotteterre family.

King Louis XIV of France had his own oboe ensemble—
The King's Twelve Excellent Oboists. Some of the twelve also played
the bassoon.

The bassoon is a big, deep-sounding double-reed instrument with
a bent tube crook called a bocal. It came along at about the same time
as the oboe and added a beautifully rich woodwind sound to the
orchestra.

bassoon double reed

bocal

bell

*Contrabassoon: Also called the double bassoon because unfolded it would be
twice the length of a bassoon, it is the largest, deepest-toned bassoon.*

left-hand keys

right-hand keys

The King's Twelve Excellent Oboists

*The bassoon has four sections of wood tubing
(usually maple) with metal joinings.*

Bassoon

The Classical Age 1750-1820

A Period of Expanding Orchestras

In the musical era called the Classical period, composers wanted orchestras that were bigger than Baroque orchestras and were capable of playing more varied and expansive music.

Franz Joseph Haydn (1732–1809) wrote more than one hundred symphonies (large-scale orchestral works usually having four sections called movements). His orchestras would typically have about twenty-five players. Instruments would include strings, oboes, bassoons, flutes, trumpets, horns, and kettledrums.

As orchestras became larger, a conductor was needed to keep everyone together and to regulate the tempo (pace) and dynamics of the music.

Crook

During this period, the large round, coiled horns made of brass were called crook horns because extra "crooks" or coils of tubing could be added to change the sets of notes the horns could play. Crooks were difficult to change quickly, though, and players often needed two or three instruments to play all the notes called for.

The longer the tubing, the lower the notes.

detachable crook tube

Kettle drums
Putting the Bomp Bomp Bah Bomp in the Orchestra

Kettledrums, also called timpani, belong to the percussion family of instruments, which provide the orchestra with rhythm, musical moods, and special effects. Kettledrums are unique, compared to other drums, because they can be "tuned" to play a specific note. The tuning can be changed by means of tension screws that tighten the drumhead to raise the note.

Although kettledrums were called for in Baroque and Classical music, it wasn't until the Romantic era that they were used to their full dramatic potential in the orchestra. Modern kettledrums use a pedal system, developed around 1850, to change the tuning more quickly.

Kettledrums are usually played in groups of two or three, each drum tuned to a different pitch. A kettledrum player is called a timpanist.

copper kettles with stretched calfskin drumheads

tuning screws

The Piano - Playing Soft and Loud

The harpsichord, with its keyboard system to pluck strings, was used prominently in the Baroque period, though its sound range is not very wide. And no matter how hard or how lightly the keys are pressed, the sound does not vary.

Around 1709, Bartolomeo Cristofori invented the pianoforte ("soft-loud" in Italian). It had a keyboard system that hit the strings with hammers to produce an expressive range of sounds—soft and loud. Today his invention is just called the piano.

In the Classical period, Wolfgang Amadeus Mozart (1756–1791) created music of extraordinary beauty and refinement for piano and orchestra.

Early keyboard instruments called spinets, virginals, clavichords, or the larger harpsichords were the result of an idea to add keys to a zither to pluck its strings. A string vibrating over the sound board produces the note.

hammers long bass strings

Although modern pianos have become larger and more powerful than Cristofori's, the basic piano shape has remained the same since 1709.

short treble (high-pitched) strings

Early pianos had only fifty to fifty-five keys, while the modern piano has eighty-eight keys.

The Romantic Period 1820-1910

The Flutes

Alto: The second highest-pitched member of an instrument family

Transverse (side-held) flutes

pads

Flute

Alto flute

Flauto piccolo

Boehm system flutes use finger key pads that cover the holes. Flutes were often made of silver, gold, or platinum.

Flauto piccolo: Means "small flute" in Italian

Bass flute

The Orchestra Grows and Grows

Improvements to instruments continued to expand the orchestra's sound with added volume, new musical tones, and sparkling effects.

In the early 1800s, many older woodwind and brass instruments were brought up to date with new machine precision. In Germany, the flute player Theobald Boehm (1794–1881) made improvements to the flute that also influenced refinements of other wind instruments. The difficult-to-play bassoon had been improved by the Heckel family. And in France, the Triébert family worked for seventy years—from 1810 to 1880—to refine the oboe.

In this period, composers often called for orchestras having more than two hundred players.

Clarinets - single reed Woodwinds

B-flat clarinet

reed

Alto clarinet

Long wood tube gives clarinets a warm, mellow tone.

Basset horn: Developed in Germany, basset horn means "little bass horn." It is not quite as large or deep in tone as the bass clarinet.

Chalumeau: single-reed pipe

The early clarinet was a chalumeau-like, single-reed instrument. In the 1840s, Hyacinthe Klosé, a clarinet teacher in Paris, borrowed many of Boehm's new flute developments and, in collaboration with the instrument maker Auguste Buffet, applied them to the clarinet.

Clarinets have a high, pleasing tone and add a rich sound to the orchestra. Although the saxophone, invented by Adolphe Sax in the early 1800s, is made of brass, it has a single reed and is related to the clarinet.

Bass clarinet

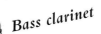

Clarinet

air slot

reed

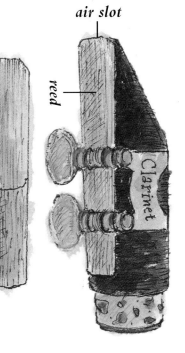

The clarinet's single reed is attached to the bottom of the mouthpiece, directly over the narrow air slot.

Blowing air causes the reed to vibrate and produce sound that is modified and expanded in the instrument.

Trombone: The standard tenor trombone is a powerful instrument that is played with seven fundamental slide positions called pedal notes.

Top Brass

Piccolo trumpet: A small trumpet that plays high, bright notes

Trumpet

Tenor horn

bell

The biggest brass instruments, the bass tubas, came into use in the 1830s.

Most brass family instruments come in a variety of sizes and can be made of metals other than brass.

Tenor: The second lowest-pitched member of an instrument family

Tuba

The Valve Invention

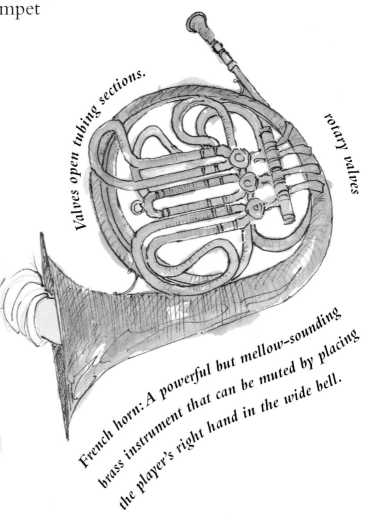

Cornet: Similar to the trumpet but with shorter, wider tubing that gives it a softer sound — side tubing

Though brass instruments had been a part of the earliest orchestras, it wasn't until the early 1800s and the application of valves to musical instruments that many of the modern brass instruments came about. During this period the tuba, tenor horn, cornet, and piccolo trumpet were invented, and the standard trumpet and French horn were redesigned to be played with valves.

Valves open tubing sections.

rotary valves

French horn: A powerful but mellow-sounding brass instrument that can be muted by placing the player's right hand in the wide bell.

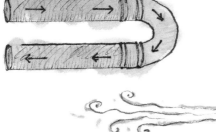

Push piston valves open and close sections of tubing to change the sound. The more tubing the vibrating air passes through, the lower the note will be. Open valve holes allow air to enter the tubing.

cornet mouthpiece

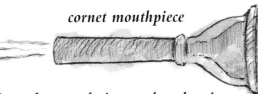

Blowing air into the mouthpiece makes the air vibrate to produce sound.

Early 1900s–A New Sound

The large modern harp, with forty-seven colored strings and seven pedals to change the tuning, is often used in the orchestra for its rich plucked-string sound.

Snare drum: A small drum with strands of wire attached across the lower drumhead which rattle when the drum is played

Snare Drum

Tom-toms

Bass drum

Innovations continued in music, as composers wanted a different sound and thus looked to new sources of inspiration. Orchestras became somewhat smaller than they had been in the Romantic period.

In his 1909–1913 orchestral work *The Rite of Spring,* the Russian-born composer Igor Stravinsky (1882–1971) used woodwinds, intense bowing of strings, and percussion to create music of vibrant rhythms and clashing tones.

More Percussion - Idiophones

Idiophones come from many different cultures and add unique sounds to the orchestra.

Xylophone: *A double row of wood or metal bars with a tube under each bar that rings a particular note when the bar is struck*

Claves

Castanets

Triangle

Tuned handbells

Cymbals

Tuned set of chimes

Rattles

Idiophone Instruments

The modern orchestra uses many percussion instruments belonging to the drum (membranophone) family—including kettledrums, bass drums, snare drums, and tom-toms—and to the idiophone family. Idiophones are instruments made of material that, when tapped, beaten, scraped, or clapped, vibrates to create sound.

"Tuned" idiophones such as xylophones and marimbas (larger, deeper-toned xylophone instruments), the celesta (a keyboard chime instrument), and sets of orchestral bells and chimes produce particular notes and can play a melody or provide special effects.

Other idiophones, such as gongs, cymbals, triangles, and claves (two small wooden sticks that are struck together), all ring with an indefinite pitch—that is, they do not hold a particular note.

Jazzy Classics
Catching the Mood

The American jazz pianist and composer Edward Kennedy "Duke" Ellington (1899–1974) was inspired by melodic, harmonic, and rhythmic elements that come from African and African American music as well as from the pulse of the modern city to form complex orchestral jazz compositions.

Jazz musicians often use their instruments in innovative ways to stretch the sound beyond the written notes and create new musical moods. This creative playing, called improvisation, along with the use of a wide range of musical tones and rhythms that can shift from "swinging" to "cool blues," characterizes jazz music.

Guitar

Tenor saxophone

The slide trombone, often used in jazz music, works as it did in Gabrieli's day.

Today-Something New

Now, as in the past, all orchestras vary somewhat in the number and mix of their instruments.

Composers today try to create fresh sounds, rhythms, and harmonies, new ways to compose music, new ways to use the instruments of the orchestra, and even ways to use a computerized synthesizer orchestra.

Software that can be used on a home computer enables you to create, process, and store your own music. The computer can compose music for you, too.

Sound modules can turn musical notes from a computer disk into a wide range of sounds.

Wind and keyboard synthesizers can modify and combine sounds.

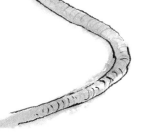

Something Old

Do not touch-
instruments
very
fragile

*Some museums that have collections
of antique instruments allow musicians
to play them for concerts.*

What Goes Around Comes Around

Some musicians and orchestras, however, look for something old to do. Today there is new interest in playing music of the past—of two, three, or four hundred years ago—on authentic instruments, that is, instruments on which the music was originally played.

A performance of Baroque music might be played with a small orchestra of viols, recorders, wooden flutes, crook horns, and a Baroque-period harpsichord.

What's Next?

No one can say what new ideas will shape the orchestras of tomorrow. We'll have to wait for that. In the meantime, perhaps orchestral music will become a part of your life: Maybe you want to hear a Baroque-period orchestra or a jazz orchestra; or maybe you want to play the oboe in your school orchestra; or maybe you just want to hear a real bassoon play.

We've seen the orchestra develop over the past four hundred years, always with a blend of ideas old and new. Without a doubt, the incredible orchestra, whatever its shape, will roll onward—to the great enjoyment of listeners along the way.